STO

ALLEN COUNTY PUBLIC LIBRARY
3 1833 00359 2315

ACPL ITEM
DISCARDED

 S0-BVP-397

JUL 22 '80

Private Lives of our Natural Neighbors

Private Lives
of our
Natural Neighbors

by
Amyas Ames

George Braziller, Inc.
New York

I pay tribute to *The Vineyard Gazette*, in which many of these essays first appeared, for it is one of the great community newspapers in this country. *The Gazette* was founded in 1846, in the days of whaling prosperity on the Vineyard, and revived by Henry Beetle Hough in 1920. It includes the world of nature in its definition of news, which is both a novel and a noble thing to do.

Copyright © 1980 by Amyas Ames
All rights reserved.
For information address the publisher:
George Braziller, Inc.
One Park Avenue
New York, N.Y. 10016

Library of Congress Cataloging in Publication Data
Ames, Amyas.
    Private lives of our natural neighbors.

    1. Natural history — Massachusetts — Martha's
Vineyard.   I.   Title.
QH105.M4A43   574.9744'94   79-6843
ISBN 0–8076–0960–9
ISBN 0–8076–0961–7 pbk.

Printed in the United States of America
First Printing
Designed by Nancy Kirsh

To Evelyn Ames
(who led me to some of these neighbors)
for her interest, her sensitivity
to nature, and her companionship.

2097641

Contents

Education of a Neighbor   9

A Tern Family   26

Monarchs Falling in for an Immense Journey   28

An Appealing Summertime Troublemaker   31

A Discerning Goldfinch with Island Tastes   32

A New Friend   34

The Graduating Class   36

Swallow Manners   38

North Tisbury Neighbors   40

Tale of a Wild Mallard   42

Off on a Dangerous Journey   44

Drama Alongshore: A Deer's Successful Flight for Life   46

Katydid   49

"Season of Mists and Mellow Fruitfulness"   50

Pasture to Forest   52

The Chance of Seeing Sanderlings   54

A Sense of Courage, Strength and Family Love   56

The Bilingual Duck   58

Jerry the Commuter   60

Observations of an Osprey Family   62

The Tree Swallow   70

A Famous Day for Spiders   74

Contemporary sculpture

Education of a Neighbor

Sixty-five years ago, as a seven-year-old boy, I started to roam the woods and ponds of my parents' land — fifteen hundred acres of deserted farms, newly grown to chestnut, oak, pine, poison ivy, and briar.

My father, a biologist, and my mother, an artist—both troubled by the bustle of the village—bought land five miles west of town and built their home. Legend has it they paid five dollars an acre, and that is a good guess inasmuch as it was the turn of the century when the New England farmer, no longer able to compete with the farmers of rich western land, deserted the old homestead to migrate or to enter the city. This land of my youth is now the Borderland State Park in Massachusetts.

My range included a powder cave of the Revolution, a three-hundred-foot "mountain" where there were rattlesnakes, and three ponds, one of over a hundred acres, accented with muskrat houses, islands and inlets. I knew the special cove where, if I approached silently, I could startle the paired woodduck, see the hollows left in the dark water from their jump, the widening rings of the tensioned surface, and hear their wild whistling call.

I came to know—with fear—the scream of the fighting coon and the struggle of nature as I roamed in the deep woods with my dog—of many breeds, but a champion in his own right. I built blinds on the little islands to watch, unseen, the life of the pond. Our pond was on a main migratory flyway from the north, a refuge on a hazardous journey, and I could hear the rapid-feathered beat of the black duck and the wild cry of the red-tailed hawk, and watch the osprey dive and lift his catch with laboring six-foot spread of wing.

During ten formative years, I learned to identify with these wild things, to sense that my mind and theirs were related. I would try to think like a duck: to sense where, if I were in flight, I would circle back over the pond; how far off the tree line I would hold for safety; which pool in the pond, and which grasses I would select; and just how I would waggle my tail once I had coasted to the end of a long, gentle splash-down. I came to believe that I knew.

I tried to think in consonance with the woodland squirrel I sometimes saw sitting upright, thoughtfully munching a mushroom held in his fore paws. I learned to slow my pace, to approach indirectly on the angled course of a passerby, not as an attacker. I would not say we had a meeting of minds, but there was much in common. The range of trust and mistrust was little different from what I later met in the megalopolis.

I left this land which we call "wild" because we are too proud to let ourselves understand that it is natural. My course took me through college, business school, the Great Depression, investment banking on Wall Street, administration in Washington, and work in the cause of the arts in a great city, a city which I love. I carried with me the sensitivity I had learned in the observation of natural things, and it served me well.

Martha's Vineyard, or perhaps more accurately the Martha's Vineyard I carry in my mind, lies in the open ocean, twenty miles east of New Bedford. It can be reached by boat from Cape Cod or by air from the mainland (if fog permits), but it is, in essence, detached from the continent of North America, inhabited by "Islanders" and, in attitude, sufficient unto itself.

It lies at that point on the eastern seaboard where two great ocean currents meet —the Labrador, cold and rich in plankton from the North, and the Gulf Stream, which brings to the Island a tempered climate friendlier than that of New England. The interplay of these currents maintains the shoals of Nantucket and Georges Bank (breeding grounds of ocean fish) and makes Martha's Vineyard the land of "Jaws," swordfish, stripers, blues, and with certain winds, the poisonous "Man-O-War."

The Vineyard's fields and surrounding waters are swept by fresher winds than elsewhere on the coast. In summer these are caused by the chill waters of Cape Cod Bay. The great hook of Cape Cod shields Martha's Vineyard from the waters of Labrador and lets warm water from the south engulf the Island. Separated by the sun-baked hook of the Cape, the two bodies of water differ in temperature by as much as 10 degrees, and this difference draws air to the Northeast, making the afternoon waters of Buzzards Bay and Vineyard Sound dance with white caps.

In other seasons, the Island is occasionally lashed by storms, designated only by compass direction by the unconcerned Islanders but often forecast as hurricanes or disasters by "off-island" radio and television. The salt spray, lifted from the surrounding waters by winds reaching over seventy knots, trims the tops of forest trees as one would trim a hedge. Some of the woodland on the Vineyard, with massive trunks over one hundred years old, are dwarfed to half-height by such pruning.

I became familiar with the unusual nature of the waters surrounding Martha's Vineyard many years ago when I first cruised in a small boat with my wife as crew.

11

"Where the wild duck nests"

Fog over the Vineyard

Cedared dew

We were young and confident navigators; however we found that what worked on the coast of Maine led to unexpected adventures south of the Cape. It was then that we read Eldridge's unsettling comments in the *Coastal Pilot:* "My extended observations on tides and tidal currents have proven that they are rendered inconstant by *distant winds,* as I have been carried out of my course on several occasions in thick weather by irregular currents (Eldridge's italics). His famous letter, repeated through the years in every issue of *The Coastal Pilot,* states:

> Do you know, Captain and Mr. Mate, of a place on the Atlantic Coast that is called "The Graveyard"? I propose to tell you something about it, and do what I can to keep vessels out of it. "The Graveyard," so called, is that part of the coast which lies between Sow and Pigs Rocks and Naushon Island. This place has been called "The Graveyard" for many years—because many a good craft has laid her bones there, and many a captain has lost his reputation there also.
> . . . . Now, as a rule, captains figure on the current, . . . as running Easterly into (Vineyard) Sound, when as a matter of fact, the first of the flood between the Lightship and Gay Head runs nearly North.

We are no longer concerned with the flow of current around Gay Head or its direction as it moves into Vineyard Sound and Buzzards Bay, for, our cruising days behind us, we have built our house on the shore overlooking the "Graveyard of the Atlantic." But these tidal currents of up to five knots are a part of Martha's Vineyard. On certain days, they can be clearly heard, as if a mountain brook were rushing over Lucas Shoal and the Middle Ground, a mile out in Vineyard Sound.

A pervasive and dramatic aspect of Martha's Vineyard is the fog which forms where the Atlantic currents meet and sweep in as a massive, gray, land-hugging cloud, bringing the beautiful blast of distant horns, the enveloping quietness of fog-muffled air, and sparkled spider webs in the cedars.

As the *Coastal Pilot* states, fog over the Vineyard tends to burn off slowly. It is this fog-laden air that encourages the thick-matted growth of lichen on trees, woodland boulders, and stone walls, and discourages the hurried mainlander as he makes his approach or departure—causing a "natural selection" of that special breed of people who love fog-bound islands.

Our home faces a meadow that, projecting as a minor point into Vineyard Sound, is graced by the flight of birds. Swallows, some nesting in our eaves, are in flight from dawn to dusk over this meadow, which also serves as a landmark for gulls returning in the evening to their colony on the dunes of Menemsha. They pass over,

l Sound

alone and in groups, sometimes complaining in flight, their slowly beating wings underlit by the setting sun. Ospreys nest on the point; marsh hawks hover in sharp inspection; and, when "the bait is in," there is the wild cry and wheeling flicker of tern fishing off the point.

Our home is in the township of North Tisbury, on the westerly side of Martha's Vineyard, a town which I would describe as a long way from New York, Boston, Edgartown and Vineyard Haven. The land of North Tisbury is sparsely settled, heavily wooded and distinguished by the lift of its hills, scoured by the melting of massive glaciers.

It was this moraine that attracted Professor Shaler, a Harvard geologist at the turn of the century. The jagged and tossed boulders of the beaches contained specimens from places as distant as Labrador, and so were ideal for teaching his students on field trips to the Island. He fell in love with the land—newly deserted sheep pasture marked with brooks, ponds, glacial holes, stone walls, sloping to the shore of Vineyard Sound—and bought close to two thousand acres, ten years before my father bought the land where I lived as a youth, forty miles to the north on the mainland.

These two Harvard professors, both scientists, knew each other. What they did not know was that their common interest in nature, one based on biology, the other on geology, would serve as a bridge for me from one land to the other.

Professor Shaler limited the use of the land, defending it from exploitation. It is now placed under a nature conservancy, and constitutes, with the adjoining land, several thousand acres of protected area—mostly forest land, but also land rich in swamps, ponds, brooks, vines, poison ivy, and briar—a refuge for natural life in this all-too-urban world.

My father, who illustrated his teaching of botany with photographs, one day bought a new camera and gave his "old" Leica to me. With the gift, came a life-long interest in photography. The picture making started with my family of four children, a subject that taught me how important the inner spirit is in a photograph. My interest evolved to include the flowers and wildlife I had come to know so well in my youth, and here, the spirit of naturalness gradually became the point of view of my pictures. The absence of quick fear, the deep inner distraction of danger, in these photographs is proof that I have attuned myself and my behavior to the nature of the wild subject.

16

*"Refuge for natural life"—
deer with fawn at evening*

Indian Pipe

18

Lady Slipper

This book—which is not concerned with people, their buildings, or their doings—treats not only of the beauty of the natural world but also of the relationship between aspects of that world and aspects of our own lives. Its pictures, as well as its text, have been influenced by a religious belief in our interconnectedness with all natural things.

When I was young in the early part of this century, I was an avid reader of Beatrix Potter and of the *Mother West Wind* stories by Thorton Burgess. I could understand and accept these writings, for my father was a biologist and we lived in the "uncivilized" countryside where there was little separation from nature. As society became more and more urban, this separation increased to the point where now it is possible not to comprehend the value of nature at all.

In the *Invisible Pyramid* Loren Eiseley writes of this deficiency as follows:

Today man's mounting numbers and his technological power to pollute his environment reveal a single demanding necessity: for him consciously to reenter and preserve, for his own safety, the old first world from which he originally emerged. His second world, drawn from his own brain, has brought him far, but it cannot take him out of nature, nor can he live by escaping into his second world alone—he must make, by use of his cultural world, an actual conscious reentry into the forest he had thought merely to exploit or abandon.

It has been my experience that the more one looks from our man-made "second world" to the "first world" of nature, the more apparent is the closeness of the two worlds. The barriers that do exist are built on prejudice and on faulty traditions of thought and language, going back to the mention of man's dominion over nature in Genesis. But such barriers can be consciously lowered, and man has much to gain in making the effort.

Friends who have read my essays have commented on the fact that I tend to *anthropomorphize*. That is a prejudicial word, part of the vocabulary of separateness that we have built up around ourselves. I see it the other way around: we do not attribute human qualities to the nonhuman—we are so totally interconnected that human qualities are available in nature for us to see. Great pleasure and, I believe, gain can be realized from freely acknowledging this interconnectedness.

These pictures were taken on Martha's Vineyard, but this is not a book about Martha's Vineyard—that just happens to be my laboratory for observation and my place for communion. Almost any other place in the country where one took the time to observe natural life would have done just as well.

20

Sweet Pepper of August

Matted growth of lichen

May Star

Wild Grape

Noman's Land—October

Storm at Gay Head

A Tern Family

"Precisely done on the wing"

The tern is one of my favorite birds. Its wild cry, to me, is the essence of the sea. Unlike the scavenger seagull, the tern is a fisherman, the great sportsman of the ocean. Fishermen on the Vineyard scorn the seagull but recognize in the tern a kindred spirit: fishing, it leads them to fish. It is sometimes called the sea swallow, and its wing-beat is so fast that the true beauty of the bird is seldom seen.

These pictures, taken on the shores of Vineyard Sound, show the hard-working parents of teenagers—young terns able to fly in an uncertain way but unable to fend for themselves. Bait was plentiful and the parents fished nearby. The young birds would watch, and when the beautiful dive of the parent was fruitful, they would turn downwind on their rock, open their beaks wide, and wait for the careful transfer of the still wriggling minnow, almost always precisely done on the wing.

"Hard-working parents"

Monarchs Falling In for an Immense Journey

Weather forecasts told us to expect a "severe chill." This translates on the Vineyard to a high-pressure area coming in from the north, bringing beautiful cool fall weather, a widening of horizons and a lift of spirit.

Although your North Tisbury observer, no doubt affected by this high, set out to see migrating shore birds on the outer beaches, he never got there: the Squibnocket uplands were alive with black and orange butterflies. It was a day for monarchs.

Each year a great company of these butterflies forms in the northeast and follows a route that crosses Martha's Vineyard on a two-thousand-mile migration south. The Squibnocket uplands, at this season a glory of goldenrod, provide them with a feast. They pause to restore their strength for the arduous crossing of the urban wasteland ahead where they find little food for butterflies.

The intentness of these monarchs on a single goldenrod indicated that they ate from a special hunger and were joined by a special spirit in their company, for although normally monarchs will not tolerate an approach within ten feet, these had no fear of a camera a foot away.

It was also clear that they played in what looked like a sense of well-being after feasting. A surge of butterflies rose over the cliff which drops two hundred feet to the surf-scoured beach and the deep blue of the Atlantic, and fell over the edge in one place to be swept by the updraft at another, repeatedly, until with a few strong wingbeats, they would return to the warm, sunlit meadowland.

As the cool of sundown began to settle, they convened in great gatherings, coming in straight and purposeful flight from as far as the eye could see, as if word of their meeting-places had been passed across the fields earlier in the day.

Although I am well aware that I cannot comprehend the mystery of a butterfly, I did sense the all-pervading spirit of adventure and migration that joined this company of monarchs.

29

"A day for monarchs"

30

"They convened in great gatherings"

An Appealing Summertime Troublemaker

"My trouble of the summer"

Here is a picture of my trouble of the summer, a young rabbit we named Peter. Our garden—so small a friend calls it a "double bed"—has always been secure behind the squares of wire shown in the picture. But this year, Peter, an unusually bright and friendly teenager, found he could crawl under the wire. That explains the boards.

With the taste of our best lettuce in his mouth, he then found he could squeeze through the square openings, although it took a strong tug to get his hind quarters through. That explains the chicken wire.

Now he comes window-shopping, and it makes me nervous.

A Discerning Goldfinch with Island Tastes

"Bee-attended thistle"

For two or three summers, we have kept our bird feeder well-stocked with thistle-seed, and, as a result, our air is filled with the color, song, and undulating flight of goldfinches. The seed we use is purchased locally but, strangely, grown in Ethiopia. Concurrently, we have had a population explosion of thistle in the meadow, which we attribute to carelessness on the part of the goldfinches.

In the fall, when this bee-attended thistle begins to fill with seed, suddenly our bountiful Ethiopian handout is deserted: the goldfinches go to the meadow and struggle endlessly for the locally grown product, filling the air with thistledown.

We cannot taste or measure the vital elements concentrated in fresh thistleseed coming from Vineyard soil, enriched by the sea, but we suspect the birds are telling us something about Island-grown food.

33

"Go to the meadow and struggle"

A New Friend

Martha's Vineyard, in the words of Henry Beston, lies "east and ahead of the Coast of North America . . . in the open Atlantic, the last fragment of an ancient and vanished land," and in the words of Barbara Chamberlin (in *These Fragile Outposts*) it is "soft, sandy and vulnerable."

Perhaps I have read too much, for I walk the beach in unease. I sense the distance down to bedrock seven hundred feet below mean highwater and wish we had the lifted base of the "stern and rockbound coast" of New England. I see the moraine, which is our lovely land yield each year to the sea—a loss, so we are told, of a foot a year over ten thousand years, now accelerated to three and one half feet a year, and predicted to be "more rapid in the future." I try to find solace in the supposed three to four thousand years it will take for my island to disappear, but that seems a short tick in time for a loved land.

I have come to see the massive rocks of the beach as friends and defenders. They emerge in steady procession from the glacial till to take their place in line for the winter wars with the sea.

Here is a portrait of my newest friend, high on the bank, a part of our reserve strength. The pictures show the lines of defense below it and to the north.

This noble rock, scooped from a valley or wrenched from a mountain as far north as Labrador, is called a "glacial erratic"—a name which suggests that geologists have faults in their terminology. The unimaginable and relentless force of the glacier easily made the Olympian effort that brought this mammoth to the farthest reach of the moraine.

As an observer of forty years, watching the rock-studded beaches and the wavering between sand and sea, I can report that on this Vineyard Sound shore the line is holding well. I find peace of mind in this resistance and sense that to forecast doom, as is man's wont, is premature here. We are rich in such mammoths as the one pictured; they are our treasures.

"Newest friend, high on the bank"

2097641

35

"Lines of defense-to the north"

The Graduating Class

"Putting on the pressure"

Parents, who worry from time to time about whether they will live to see their children mature, may take comfort from this picture of a North Tisbury family.

At first glance this group of seniors (they graduated next day) seems to be the chorus of the Glee Club, singing a cappella. In fact, they are just putting on the pressure for more food.

The parents, who grace our home and meadow, work from dawn until dark, when they seem to be guided to bugs by some miracle of night vision.

The next day after watching the swallow graduation exercises, we consulted our Forbush, *Birds of Massachusetts and Other New England States* (1929). It states: "Most of the individuals of the first brood probably leave for the seashore in August . . . . The male usually cares for the first brood after they are well able to fly and until they learn to catch their own food; meanwhile the female prepares for the second brood."

This is what the swallows of North Tisbury do to raise their families, and as long as they can do it, perhaps we can too.

"Singing a cappella"

Swallow Manners

As a parent of four, I have always felt deep sympathy for the swallows who work to keep ahead of the baby birds' hunger and are confronted, as they bring food, by that straining row of hexagonal bills, suddenly agape in the nest. I worry about all those decisions regarding which hole to fill, how to be fair, how to help the weakest, and restrain the most aggressive.

This series of pictures of this year's family, taken early on the morning the young left the nest, show that the parents have established a family procedure, and that the young are well on the way to learning manners. I find this reassuring in our world which tends to emphasize disorder, and worthy of fuller explanation.

The first evidence of parental control is that, after the heady excitement of the first flight from the nest, the four young teenagers have been gathered together on the back of one of our outdoor chairs.

Notice in the next picture how, while the bird on the left is being fed, the second and third are quiet, even looking the other way. The fourth youngster is clearly establishing his right to be next.

And above notice how, while the fourth bird is being fed, number three is establishing a position, lifting off the perch in anticipation. Numbers one and two merely watch.

The feeding is then slowed by an aborted mission, caused by the difficult position of number three, perched downwind within an inch of the chair bar. The

epiglottal delivery was completed with great grace, as shown in the last picture in this sequence. Meanwhile, in that picture, number two is calling for his allotted turn and number one, overcome by the slowness of the whole procedure, has sunk into a dejection, verging on despair.

As you may have guessed, number two received his fare on the next fly-by.

North Tisbury Neighbors

We have been fortunate enough to watch a happy event here in North Tisbury: the birth of four healthy garter snakes.

My naturalist-inclined son encountered a snake on the edge of a little pond in the woods and noticed that it looked gravid (i.e., pregnant), with a long swelling forward of its vent. Urged by his children, he put it temporarily into an old aquarium with some oak leaves, lichens, sticks and a bowl of water. He included a small frog, which the snake ate, and the first picture is a portrait of "garter snake contentment."

I should say that my wife, Evelyn, and I are somewhat acquainted with snakes. She knows a large one that is always lying at the doorway of her writing studio: she talks to it daily. And there is a small snake who watches me work in the garden and whom I look upon as a friend. But neither of us knew that garter snakes are viviparous (i.e. born, not hatched).

Two days later two baby snakes were born, followed by two more the next day. The process was complete with umbilical cords and afterbirths and what my grandchildren called "see-through" sacs. The babies were a little over four inches long at birth and seemed to grow steadily thereafter. The second picture shows one of the babies — not much more than the length of a forest leaf.

Just before we released the family there was a moment of high drama. The mother had seemed relaxed, eating two more frogs and a salamander in the two days after giving birth to her babies. Suddenly, she came directly toward my camera lens, forked tongue darting in and out, her whole body tensed to strike, in a flare of protective anger (third picture). She had seen in the reflecting lens of my camera what she took to be another snake.

When released, the mother moved with an almost dignified slowness into the pond. The babies explored gingerly, and then, driven by instinct, sought cover in the forest leaves.

"Garter snake contentment"

"Length of a forest leaf"

"Flare of anger"

41

Tale of a Wild Mallard

In a small pond, in the woods close to Vineyard Sound, is a heavily grassed island, perhaps twice as big as a livingroom rug — perfectly suited to our five and seven-year-old grandchildren in their red rubber boat.

A project was developed to cut the grass on the island, and, in the process we uncovered a nest with eleven big eggs. The mother, a wild mallard, returned to her partly exposed nest, and from then on the grandchildren could watch developments. There was no drake, and it made us all sad that our mother duck had been deserted.

The big day came—a day of rejoicing—and here is a picture of our duck with her nine babies swimming close to the little island.

But our joy was shortlived: later that same day they all disappeared, leaving us with visions of attacks by turtles, hawks, foxes, or worse.

I consulted our Forbush, and here is what I found out about mallards:

The Mallard will breed almost anywhere if unmolested. Its adaptability has made it the chief wild duck of the world. It will nest on a little islet in a small pond — near a boiler factory [even near grandchildren!].

When incubation begins, the male, like most other ducks when thus left to their own devices, deserts the female and seeks only his own comfort and pleasure, leaving the mother to care for the young. [As the saying goes, "it figures."]

It feeds readily on land and requires very little water. If food conditions are not satisfactory where they are hatched, the mother leads them overland to other waters.

Apparently, our North Tisbury mallard was raising her family in the tradition of her forebears, and all our fears were groundless.

"The big day came"

Off on a Dangerous Journey

"Her course set, her head held high"

Twenty-four hours ago, these wild mallard ducklings were in the egg. Now, drawn close together for safety, the family is in an alert — caused by a passing dog whose barking from the shoreline led the mother to scream her defiance in duck language.

This is the second year the mother has chosen to nest on a small, thickly grassed island in this brook-fed pond in the woods. Somehow, although our grandchildren play there, she has kept her presence on the island secret for twenty-six days.

According to Forbush, these day-old ducks are able to dive and, when endangered, to hide, either beneath the surface or amidst the water plants, with only the bill above water. Truly this is a miracle of natural "programming."

As she did last year, the mother is taking her day-old family to waters that are safer or better supplied with food. Beset by the threat of great snapping turtles, dogs, feral cats, coon, hawks, and owls, this dangerous journey will not end until migration is completed in the fall. It takes tight discipline to bring a family through safely, but, as the picture show, she has it. Her course set, her head held high, our North Tisbury duck is on her way.

"Drawn close together for safety"

Drama Alongshore: A Deer's Successful Flight for Life

"She swam, unflustered and confident"

My grandson Ethan was fishing on the shore of Vineyard Sound when he saw a deer run from the woods about one-quarter of a mile away, take the beach in one leap, and hurl herself into the water. There was a fair sea running at the time, and she made a great splash as she hit the first wave.

She had been driven to this desperate tactic by the relentless chase of two dogs. She swam straight into the Vineyard Sound for about three hundred yards before she turned south, setting a course parallel to the shore where my grandson stood.

He is a fast runner and set out for home where I was playing cards with his sister. He banked the corner of the open door on one solidly placed Addidas and shouted, "There is a deer swimming in Vineyard Sound." Then, he grabbed my binoculars

"Leaping to avoid the tumble of the waves"

and ran out. I yelled at him to put the binocular strap over his head and turned to his sister to ask what he had said. "There is a deer swimming in Vineyard Sound," she repeated.

Our playing cards spread all over the floor, we raced to the bluff and saw the deer, head high, showing the well-established wake of a strong swimmer (first picture). She swam—or so I firmly believe—on a preset course, obviously unflustered and confident.

Her swim, measured from hoofprints-in to hoofprints-out, was five-eighths of a mile long. At about the halfway mark, she altered course, angling to meet the beach one-quarter of a mile away. She seemed to take a bearing on the next point, and later we did find a well-tracked deer path there.

"She came up the beach with her ears held high"

As she came out, she showed her experience by leaping to avoid the tumble of the waves, letting them roll under her (second picture). Then, she came up the beach to return to familiar paths with her ears held high.

I have been told since by friends, learned in the ways of the Vineyard wild, that deer often take to the water to avoid dogs. In each of the two cases reported to me, they swam straight out for about three hundred yards and circled until the dogs, unknowing, noses down, checked the beach and returned to the woods, trying to find where their mistake had been made. But sometimes, in the dead of winter, deer do not get back before the cold saps their strength. Then, their bones may be found on the shore.

Katydid

Katydids are heard but seldom seen, for they sing in the trees and only at night. Here, by happy chance, is one of our North Tisbury katydids — out early in the waning light of the setting sun.

The katydid is a noted songster, intoning the mood of fall. The tempo of its rhythmic call varies with the temperature, becoming slower with cold: one can tell by an ear to the window whether or not one needs a sweater.

The male, who is the singer, rubs a sharp edge of one wing over a file-like ridge on the other. The sound produced helps one katydid find another in the dark of the wood.

"Season of Mists and Mellow Fruitfulness"

Butternut

One might think it a giant step from a North Tisbury butternut to Keats, but these pictures reminded my wife Evelyn of the ode "To Autumn," and the season that "fill(s) all fruit with richness to the core . . . and plump(s) the hazel shells with a sweet kernel . . .".

By some alchemy of extreme cold, high winds, heavy rains and sun-filled dry spells, this year has produced one of the most fruitful seasons in recent memory.

Peterson's *Field Guide to Trees* tells us that oak fruits form a large portion of the food consumed by game birds and mammals; that sassafras fruits are eaten by songbirds, bob-white, and wild turkey; that the fleshy bitter fruits of beetlebung are relished by more than thirty species of birds; and that the Indians boiled the butternut to obtain oil for use as butter. It does not mention what a treasure they are to squirrels, mice, and others.

With winter not far away, it is good to know that this year's unusually bountiful crop has made our Island's woods so rich in food.

Tupelo

Oak

51

Pasture to Forest

Martha's Vineyard was a land of pastures one hundred years ago. Henry Hough wrote that: it "was crosshatched by stone walls that surmounted the hills and were silhouetted against the sky, looking like the fancy filament of a queen's crown, and adding not a little to the landscape." With the decline of sheep-grazing and farming, many of those pastures have given way to trees, and the stone walls that delineated them now run through woodland.

I began to understand the life cycle of trees on an Arbor Day sixty-five years ago when I planted the first of many saplings. Now, when I forget my age, I have the massive trunks of those lofty giants to remind me.

I did not see the first stage when the pastures became scrub land (although some of my friends did), nor the second stage when the hard-wood started; but I have watched the steady growth in recent years. This picture shows that what was once pasture and then woods is now forest. In some areas—North Tisbury for example— our forest trees have taken on girth and grandeur rivaling the finest in New England.

"Stone walls now run through woodland"

The Chance of Seeing Sanderlings

"Trace the tideline darkly"

The light of late afternoon laces everything with shadow, increasingly so as the sun nears the horizon; and shadows, whether on waves or on sanderlings, emphasize contour. It is the time of day best suited to see the shape of things.

Here, with the sparkle of a brilliant day still alive on the crests of the waves, here with the shadows of the merry little sanderlings' wings on the sand indicating the position of the sun, the spindrift's folds trace the tide line darkly. Night will come. It is the time to see the sanderlings on the outer beaches, even though it will be dark before one gets home.

A Sense of Courage, Strength and Family Love

These geese chose a small, wild pond close to Vineyard Sound in North Tisbury to bring up their brood of goslings. It is not surprising that they were there, for Forbush tells us that the early explorers found geese nesting on the islands along the coast of Massachusetts.

Watching this family, I was impressed by the parents, the closeness, and the sense of discipline. Perhaps that is why all six goslings were still alive. They seemed to understand that danger increases with the diameter of the family circle, and so the young were kept close.

I hope these pictures convey the courage, strength, and family love which I saw that day.

"Courage, strength, and family love"

The Bilingual Duck

We are often told of research on the language of birds; a recent New York Times article concluded: "They have a language just as we do." Judging by the *Times* article, the scientists are focusing thus far on language within a bird family; but it is likely, as this story of an event in North Tisbury attests, that there is language communication between species as well.

The bilingual duck of my report raises her brood in a secret place on an island in a little woodland pond about one-quarter of a mile from our house. You, the reader, have met her previously in "Tale of a Wild Mallard," and "Off on a Dangerous Journey."

Up the hill and through the woods from the pond, right in front of our house, stands a large cedar tree, its branches winter-trimmed by deer. There, we keep a birdfeeder filled with thistleseed. In the years that we have been doing this, we have never seen a duck on our lawn, certainly not at the feeder, nor have we ever seen our wild duck fly over, as her normal approach to her nest is beyond the woods one-quarter of a mile away.

This year, due to disturbances in Ethiopia, our source of thistleseed dried up, forcing us to use a more mundane mixture which contained cracked corn. This new food was not to the liking of the birds: the first day's consumption dropped to about one-third and the goldfinches deserted in a flock.

The next day the nesting mallard duck appeared, circled the house, landed on the lawn, and waddled very cautiously to the corn scattered under the feeder. Each morning thereafter, at about eight thirty, when the cool of night no longer endangered her eggs, she flew back, gaining a little more confidence and a little more corn as we increased her ration.

I believe that sitting in quiet on her nest, she had heard the complaints of the birds as they came to water at the edge of the pond, informing her of the change in our feeder and, perhaps, of food fit for a duck.

Testing this theory with those learned in letters and science, I find them skeptical about communication among birds: perhaps they are touched by the hubris of mankind. Testing this theory with those learned in the ways of nature, I find a quick acceptance. To our North Tisbury duck, it is all self-evident.

Jerry the Commuter

When my wife Evelyn, coming in from a walk, told of seeing a muskrat in one of the little glacier-scoured ponds close to Vineyard Sound, I went to watch him from under a blueberry bush on the bank. He is "Jerry the commuter." He is "Jerry" because I have never known a muskrat by any other name, and "the commuter" because, after thirty-five years on the Long Island Railroad, I know one when I see one.

I watched him for five round trips, or the equivalent of a week's commuting. It was all there: the air of determination, head down; the well-established pressure wave; the briefcase of neatly arranged grasses carried in his mouth; the expectation of home and a loving family. On each westerly trip, he would lift out of the water as the bottom rose to meet him, shake, and disappear along the little path tunneled through the grasses, headed for the succulent spring growth back from the edge of the pond. In about five minutes, he would be back, sink into the water, and swim out across the pond. I do not know whether the grasses (always arranged with Swiss-like precision) were building material or muskrat salad for a busy mother, but I do know that he cared.

"The Commuter: "well-established pressure wave"

Observations On An Osprey Family

The male: "smaller but a fine provider"

Two years ago the adult ospreys of these pictures started as teenagers to build their first nest. They chose our pole, designed as a nesting site by the director of the Felix Neck Wildlife Trust. The scaffolding we provided was an upended oak stump with roots outspread, bolted to an old telephone pole, and mounted near the shores of Vineyard Sound.

The first year only half of the nest was finished since our newly mated birds spent more time flying around and fishing than building a home. The second year their two eggs hatched, but either because of raccoons or the great storm of that June, the fledglings were lost.

In their third attempt, the family has met with success. This year, protected by a

The female: "circling closely to scold an intruder"

metal raccoon guard, their nest almost doubled in size, and they have raised their family. We could observe them from a particular window or from the roof of our house, and these pictures relate what we saw.

The female cared for and guarded her young, rarely leaving the nest except to circle closely and scold an intruder. Her cheeping was so frequently heard, on occasion even at night, that a mockingbird echoed it from the bushes.

In marked contrast to her mate, who finished eating before he would share his catch, she always fed her young before herself. She would tear off bite-size pieces of the freshly caught fish—the sole food of the osprey—and hold them gently out to each of her two babies in turn.

"Long legs, powerful claws"

On hot days she would spread her immense wings over the nest to shade her fledglings, holding this seemingly awkward position for three or four hours at a time. In a similar manner, she would protect the young from the cold of rain until they were almost grown.

Her discipline over her family was absolute, so that the fledglings dropped immediately out of sight in the cavernous nest at the first warning cry. Her total immersion in the care of her young seemed a miracle of motherhood.

With the mother and babies in the nest there was no room for the male, so he chose a protruding root (we called it "the front porch") for his favorite perch. Somewhat smaller than his mate, he was a fine provider for his family, and an excellent fisherman.

The osprey is a very strong bird with unusually long legs, powerful claws, and a reversible outer toe adapted to catching and holding fish. In the photograph above, a

"To freshen the wall-to-wall carpeting"

hornpout from a nearby pond is carried head foremost by the bird who extends his right leg for a one-foot landing.

Our ospreys always ate on the edge of the nest and always, if disturbed while eating, took their meal with them into the air.

In the evening, after the family was fed, the male would usually catch one more fish and swing within a few yards of the nest, apparently to show his family his evening snack, on the way to a more protected nighttime perch.

Maintenance and improvement of the nest was a constant concern of the parents. In the photograph above, note how the female, to the obvious interest of her family, brings a fresh supply to dry seaweed to freshen the wall-to-wall carpeting. As the young became more independent, the parents devoted more time to collecting freshly broken sticks, perhaps to reinforce and strengthen the nest against the winter storms.

Flight exercises

From time to time visitors from elsewhere on the Island would circle over the nest as if interested in the progress of the family. Our osprey were always very alert and would not let their neighbors come too close. The male rose from the nest directly under the visiting bird in order to enforce a territorial barrier, while the female spread her protective wings over the young.

The climax of these visits came one beautiful, windless day when the young were almost grown and engaged in the flapping exercise of youth. Eight great birds came to call in the late afternoon, and the parents rose to join them in a ceremonial circling high in the evening sky.

The flapping stage of the young osprey is one of unceasing, almost chaotic activity on the nest. Surveyed constantly by the mother who retreats to the edge to

"Their mother circles in attendance"

make room, the young birds, with viselike grips on one of the stronger sticks, wave their seemingly too large wings in a prolonged beating. After several days they venture to lift their feet, becoming airborne, only to grab quickly for the stick — much like a young bicyclist trying to ride no-hands. Later, a growing confidence lets them lift their long legs all the way up and hover for a few seconds over the center of the nest.

The day of our young ospreys' first flight seemed chosen for the occasion, clear and bright, with a steady morning wind and both parents in attendance. The young birds, each in turn, lifted slowly over the nest and flew off in a circle, which widened as the day went on. They came back for an upwind landing, which deteriorated as they came over the nest into what looked like a desperate clutch. They watched their

"Designed as a nesting site"

mother circle in attendance, and their interest intensified as she demonstrated the art of approach, settling gently to the edge of the nest with every flight feather spread to the cushioning air (upper picture page 69).

We had ample time to witness the learning process: the wrong way to make such an approach is on page 69. A young bird makes three mistakes in a single attempt: the approach to the nest was too high; the hovering technique to recover from such a mistake was too late; and the attempt to fly backwards (obviously a mistake) failed, as the bird, legs extended, looks back at the missed target. The others can't bear to watch. As soon as the flying lessons are over, fishing lessons will begin—the next step in preparation for the fall migration.

According to the census conducted by the Wildlife Trust, thirteen young birds in six nests have been raised on Martha's Vineyard this year. Five other nests are in formation and can be expected to have young osprey next year. Only a few years ago, before the use of the hard pesticide DDT was banned by federal law, the osprey was close to extinction on Martha's Vineyard. We can be thankful that affairs have been so ordered that ospreys such as these proud parents are once again able to raise their stalwart young.

The Art of Landing: Pupil

Tree swallow

The Tree Swallow:

This tree swallow—a people watcher—dropped out of his wheeling flight to take an intent look at the photographer, busy in the warmth of early morning sunlight.

Tree swallows differ from barn swallows in that their breast is wholly white, their nest is built, lined with warm feathers, in a cavity such as a woodpecker hole, bird house, or mailbox, and their food includes more vegetable matter, mainly wild berries and seeds, allowing them to arrive earlier in the spring and to leave later in the fall.

Forebush, in one of my favorite passages on the tree swallow, writes: "As with mankind, it seems that their conjugal affairs do not always go well. Inconstancy is a failing common to birds as well as men." He then reports the observations of three women who were accustomed to sit under a hollow apple tree in which a pair of tree swallows had built their nest:

> As their seat was directly opposite the nest hole, they could watch the devoted husband bringing food to his mate in the nest. To their surprise during one of his absences, another tree swallow, apparently an immature male with a brownish back, came to the hole and began to chatter to the female inside. She came to her door and opened a conversation with her caller, who when her husband returned, beat a hurried retreat. This happened again and again. If the husband returned unexpectedly and found the stranger in close communion with his mate, he fell upon the interloper furiously, while the unfaithful wife chatted excitedly in her doorway. Finally, one day she was seen to come out and fly away with the stranger, never to return. Her mate mourned for a day and then he, too, disappeared, leaving the eggs cold in the deserted nest.

Although the photograph entitled "The Hussy (three's a crowd)" clearly indicates the threat of such a sad breakup, this pair would seem to be well-mated, and one suspects the intruder failed in his attempt.

Mated

A Problem

Solved

72

The Hussy (three's a crowd)

Two Points of View

One

A Famous Day For Spiders

Early in the lovely month of September, a day dawned when everything was perfect for spiders, as it was for us.

I was up early that morning and found their spinnakers set in the cedars, trimmed to catch the gentle drift of northerly air, lit by the rising sun. Trees, webs, and grass sparkled in heavy dew. It was a display of beauty unparalleled in my memory.

My library is not very informative on spiders, but I have found a passage in Guy Murchie's *The Seven Mysteries of Life: An Exploration of Science and Philosophy,* from which I quote the following:

> The spider spins a circular web, not with eyesight but by feel and instinct, usually in the darkness before dawn, measuring and adding a new ring to the orb every second, the whole taking less than half an hour. Though indelibly fixed in their genes, the designs [of spider webs] outwardly express the spider's inward moods and minds, being somehow influenced by every environment factor from weather to diet.

Mr. Murchie tells of experiments with diet: if you give a spider a little coffee, "his next web will be a loose ragged array of unfinished spokes."

Although my experience with spiders is limited to collisions with their webs on woodland paths and to startled encounters with large, if friendly, ones in the house, I can imagine their day-to-day problems. Their webs can be battered by rain, torn by wind, exposed by beads of fog, and shattered by birds and passersby not attuned to their finery.

These pictures show what happens to a spider's mood in the dead of night when all the environmental factors fall into place. It was a perfect day for spiders, and these were some of the webs spun from their ebullience, in celebration.